Retire Rich

Planning for a Comfortable Retirement

Robert M. Watson

Disclaimer

The information provided in this book is for general informational purposes only and is not intended to be, and should not be taken as, financial, investment, or legal advice. The author and publisher of this book are not financial advisors and do not endorse or recommend any particular investment or financial strategy.

Investing involves risk, including the risk of loss. The value of your investments may fluctuate and you may lose money. Past performance is not indicative of future results. It is important to carefully consider your financial goals, risk tolerance, and other personal factors before making any investment decisions.

You should consult with a financial professional before making any investment decisions and carefully review all relevant documents, including prospectuses, before investing. The author and publisher of this book are not responsible for any errors or omissions, or for any actions taken based on the information contained in this book.

This book is not a substitute for professional financial advice and should not be relied upon as such. The author and publisher of this book do not guarantee the accuracy, completeness, or usefulness of the information contained in this book and will not be liable for any errors or omissions, or for any actions taken based on the information contained in this book.

Contents

Chapter 1: The Importance of Retirement Planning

Introduction

Retirement. The mere mention of the word conjures up visions of relaxing beach holidays, endless rounds of golf, and spending quality time with loved ones. However, the serene, carefree lifestyle that we all aspire to enjoy in our later years doesn't just magically happen. It is the result of deliberate, careful, and often complex planning. Without proper retirement planning, the dream of a comfortable retirement can easily turn into a stressful reality.

Retirement planning is the process of determining your retirement income goals and the necessary actions to achieve them. Essentially, it involves evaluating your current financial standing and devising an effective strategy that will ensure your financial security during retirement. When done correctly, it allows for the maintenance of the lifestyle you've grown accustomed to even after you've stopped working.

However, planning for retirement isn't solely about securing your financial future; it is about paving the way to a life of fulfillment and purpose. It's about shaping your golden years in a way that aligns with your vision of personal happiness and satisfaction.

As you embark on your retirement planning journey, it's important to understand the gravity of the task at hand. It isn't a matter of simply saving a certain percentage of your income every month. Rather, it is an ongoing process that requires timely revisions, smart decision-making, and a thorough understanding of various financial instruments and investment strategies.

This chapter aims to underscore the significance of retirement planning. It seeks to shed light on the reasons why it should be considered an indispensable component of your financial plan. And in doing so, it will pave the way for you to cultivate a solid foundation upon which to build the rest of this book's subsequent chapters.

In the following pages, we will delve into the primary reasons why retirement planning is so essential. From outliving your savings due to increased life expectancy, to dealing with the risk of inflation, to coping with unexpected health care costs, to navigating the ever-changing landscape of government benefits – the reasons are as numerous as they are compelling.

Embrace this chapter as a wake-up call - a call to take control, to strategize, and to effectively plan for your retirement. It is a call to action that could lead to the comfortable, secure retirement you've always dreamed of. By understanding and appreciating the importance of retirement planning, you are taking the first and perhaps most crucial step towards retiring rich.

And isn't that the dream we all share? Let us begin the journey.

Explanation of Why Planning for Retirement is Crucial

In our ever-evolving world, the importance of planning for retirement cannot be overstated. With changes in socio-economic dynamics, the traditional safety nets once provided by both government and employers have become increasingly uncertain. As a result, the onus is on us, the individuals, to ensure our own financial security in retirement. Here are several compelling reasons why planning for retirement is crucial:

Increased Life Expectancy:

Due to advancements in healthcare, people are living longer, healthier lives. While this is undoubtedly a positive trend, it also means that the period of retirement is increasing. The longer you live, the more money you will need to sustain your lifestyle. Without a well-thought-out retirement plan, there is a serious risk of outliving your savings, leading to financial hardships in your twilight years.

Rising Healthcare Costs:

The cost of healthcare is increasing at a rate faster than inflation. As we age, we become more susceptible to health problems, making healthcare expenses a significant part of our retirement budget.

Adequate retirement planning takes into account these inevitable costs, allowing you to live comfortably without the fear of medical expenses draining your savings.

Uncertainty of Social Security:

The Social Security system was established to provide a safety net for retirees. However, with the ratio of workers to retirees decreasing, the sustainability of Social Security benefits is uncertain. By planning for retirement, you're not solely reliant on this source of income to fund your golden years.

Impact of Inflation:

Inflation can erode the purchasing power of your savings. A loaf of bread that costs $2 today could cost significantly more in 20 or 30 years. Your retirement plan should account for inflation to maintain your purchasing power and provide a comfortable lifestyle.

Desire for Financial Independence:

Retirement is the culmination of years of hard work and can be a time to pursue interests and hobbies that were sidelined during working years. Proper planning enables you to have the financial independence to enjoy this phase of life without the burden of financial worry.

The Need to Leave a Legacy:

Many individuals wish to leave behind a financial legacy for their children, grandchildren, or charitable causes. By including estate planning in your retirement plan, you ensure that your wishes are met after your lifetime.

To conclude, retirement planning is no longer a luxury; it is a necessity. It's about preparing for the longest holiday of your life. By understanding these crucial factors and incorporating them into your retirement plan, you set the stage for a fulfilling and financially secure retirement.

Discussing Common Misconceptions About Retirement Planning**

Retirement planning can often be clouded by misconceptions and misguided notions that can derail even the most well-intentioned plans. Let's unpack some of the most common myths that can pose significant roadblocks on your journey to a prosperous retirement:

Misconception: Retirement Planning is Only for the Elderly:

Many people believe that retirement planning is a task to be tackled in their later years. However, this approach could significantly reduce your potential savings. The earlier you start planning for retirement, the more time your money has to grow, thanks to the power of compound interest.

Misconception: I Will Spend Less When I Retire:

While it's true that some costs, like commuting or work clothes, will disappear, others, such as healthcare or hobbies, can increase. Furthermore, inflation continues to raise the cost of living. Assuming you'll spend less could result in a shortfall of funds when you retire.

Misconception: My Social Security Benefits Will be Enough:

While Social Security can provide a base of income, it's unlikely to be enough to sustain your lifestyle fully. Depending on Social Security benefits as your primary source of income could result in a lower standard of living than anticipated.

Misconception: My Employer's Pension or Retirement Plan Will Cover My Needs:

While employer-sponsored plans can form a vital part of your retirement savings, relying solely on them could be risky. Changes in the economic environment, company fortunes, and plan provisions could affect your retirement funds. It's best to diversify your retirement savings across multiple sources.

Misconception: Medicare Will Cover All My Health Costs:

Medicare does not cover all health expenses. Costs related to dental, vision, long-term care, and certain prescription drugs are typically out-of-pocket expenses. Underestimating healthcare costs in retirement can significantly impact your savings.

Misconception: I'm Too Late to Start Saving for Retirement:

While starting early is beneficial, it's never too late to start planning for retirement. Every bit of saving and investing helps. You can take advantage of catch-up contributions allowed in many retirement plans for those over a certain age.

By dispelling these misconceptions, you gain a clearer, more accurate understanding of retirement planning. Remember, the journey towards a comfortable retirement begins with a single step: start planning today. The future 'you' will thank you for the foresight and prudence you exercised today.

How Retirement Planning Has Evolved Over Time

The concept of retirement, and consequently retirement planning, has undergone a profound transformation over the decades. What started as a safety net for the old and infirm has morphed into a long-anticipated life stage, replete with dreams of travel, leisure, and personal fulfillment. This evolution has been driven by various socio-economic factors and technological advancements.

Early 20th Century - The Birth of Retirement:

Retirement, as a distinct life phase, began to take shape with the advent of Social Security in the 1930s. Initially, it was designed as a safeguard against the societal problem of the aged being left in poverty, offering support for those who could no longer work. Retirement planning was virtually non-existent since life expectancies were shorter, and people often worked until they physically could not.

Mid to Late 20th Century - The Golden Age of Pensions:

The post-World War II era saw the rise of defined-benefit pension plans offered by employers. Workers could look forward to retiring with a guaranteed income for life, dependent on their salary and years of service. Retirement planning was largely a matter of staying with one employer long enough to qualify for a pension.

Late 20th Century - The Shift to Self-Reliance:

In the late 20th century, two significant shifts occurred. First, life expectancies began to rise dramatically, meaning retirement savings had to last for a longer period. Second, employers began moving away from defined-benefit pensions to defined-contribution plans, like 401(k)s. This shift transferred the responsibility of retirement savings from the employer to the employee, marking the dawn of modern retirement planning.

21st Century - The Rise of Individual Responsibility and Technology:

In the 21st century, retirement planning has become a complex process requiring individual initiative. With longer lifespans, the potential insufficiency of social security, and increasing healthcare costs, planning for retirement has become a critical aspect of personal finance. The rise of technology has made financial information and investment platforms more accessible, empowering individuals to take control of their retirement planning.

The Future - Holistic and Personalized Planning:

The future of retirement planning is evolving towards a more holistic, personalized approach. It's not just about financial planning anymore. It's about lifestyle planning - aligning one's financial resources with their vision of retirement. The integration of AI and big data in financial planning tools is enabling more customized and predictive retirement strategies, helping individuals make better-informed decisions.

In essence, retirement planning has evolved from being a passive expectation to an active process that requires ongoing engagement. Understanding this evolution not only gives us a glimpse into how far we've come, but also offers insights into how we can prepare for what lies ahead. It reinforces the fact that retirement planning is not a one-size-fits-all proposition, but a highly personal journey that can lead to a fulfilling and financially secure retirement.

Chapter 2: Understanding Your Financial Status

Evaluating Current Financial Status

Before you set sail on your retirement planning journey, it's essential to understand your point of departure - your current financial status. Knowing where you stand financially today provides a clear snapshot of your economic health, helping you to set realistic goals for your future and map out a path to achieve them. Here's how you can perform a comprehensive evaluation of your current financial status:

Calculate Your Net Worth:

Your net worth is the difference between what you own (assets) and what you owe (liabilities). Assets include savings, investments, real estate, and personal property. Liabilities include mortgage debt, car loans, credit card debt, and any other obligations. Calculating your net worth gives you an overall picture of your current financial standing and provides a baseline for tracking your financial progress over time.

Assess Your Income and Expenses:

Understanding your cash flow - the money that comes in and goes out - is a critical part of financial planning. This involves tallying up all sources of income and contrasting them with all your expenses, both fixed and variable. By doing this, you will get a clear picture of how much money you're able to save each month and identify areas where you can potentially cut back to save more.

Understand Your Debt:

Debt can significantly impact your retirement plans. High-interest debt, like credit card debt, can eat into your savings, hindering your ability to grow wealth for retirement. Calculate the total amount of your outstanding debts, the associated interest rates, and your monthly payments. This will aid in devising a strategy to pay off your debt as quickly as possible.

Evaluate Your Investments:

Take stock of all your current investments, including retirement accounts, stocks, bonds, mutual funds, real estate, etc. Evaluate their performance and how they align with your retirement goals. It's crucial to understand your risk tolerance and ensure your investment strategy reflects that.

Review Your Insurance Coverage:

Insurance plays a crucial role in protecting your financial plan. It's essential to review your insurance policies (health, life, disability, home, auto) to ensure they offer adequate coverage. As we age, our insurance needs change, and so should our coverage.

Consider Your Tax Situation:

Taxes can significantly impact your retirement savings. Understanding your current tax situation can help you identify opportunities to save more effectively. This could involve strategies like contributing to tax-advantaged retirement accounts or considering tax-efficient investments.

Conducting a comprehensive evaluation of your current financial status may seem daunting, but it's a crucial step in effective retirement planning. It provides a solid foundation upon which you can build your financial future. Remember, it's not about where you start; it's about where you're heading and taking the right steps to get there.

Understanding Net Worth

At the heart of your financial status lies a key figure: your net worth. This figure is a snapshot of your financial health at a given point in time and a metric that can track your financial progress throughout your life. Understanding your net worth is fundamental to both financial planning and setting realistic retirement goals.

What is Net Worth?

Net worth is the difference between your total assets and total liabilities. In other words, it represents what you own minus what you owe. It's the financial value that you would be left with if you sold all your assets and paid off all your debt.

How to Calculate Net Worth?

Calculating your net worth involves two main steps:

First, total up all your assets. These can include:

- Cash and cash equivalents like checking and savings accounts
- Investments such as stocks, bonds, mutual funds, and retirement accounts
- Real estate properties
- Personal property of value, such as cars, jewelry, or collectibles

Next, total up all your liabilities, which could include:

- Mortgages
- Car loans
- Student loans
- Credit card debt
- Any other outstanding loans or financial obligations

Subtract your total liabilities from your total assets to calculate your net worth:

Net Worth = Total Assets - Total Liabilities

Why is Net Worth Important?

Your net worth is a key indicator of your financial stability and health. A positive net worth means that you own more than you owe, which indicates financial strength. A negative net worth, on the other hand, indicates that you owe more than you own, signaling potential financial vulnerability.

Moreover, tracking your net worth over time allows you to gauge your financial progress. Growing net worth is generally a sign that you're moving in the right direction - accumulating assets and reducing debts. It can also help highlight areas that need improvement, such as excessive debt.

Using Net Worth for Retirement Planning:

In the context of retirement planning, your net worth can guide you in setting retirement savings goals and timelines. It helps in determining how much you will need to maintain your desired lifestyle in retirement and provides a baseline for measuring progress towards your retirement goals.

Understanding your net worth is the starting line for your journey towards financial planning and retirement readiness. It's a numerical representation of your financial decisions - past and present, and serves as a compass, helping you navigate towards a financially secure retirement.

The Role of Debt in Financial Planning

Debt plays a complex role in financial planning. While too much debt can impede your financial goals and become a source of stress, strategic use of certain types of debt can be a powerful tool in wealth building. The key lies in understanding the nature of your debt and managing it effectively.

Understanding Good Debt and Bad Debt:

All debt is not created equal. It can be broadly classified into two categories: good debt and bad debt.

Good Debt: This is debt that can potentially generate long-term income or increase your net worth. Mortgages, student loans, or business loans can be examples of good debt. A mortgage can help you acquire a home, a valuable asset, and student loans can fund an education that increases your earning potential.

Bad Debt: This is debt incurred to purchase things that quickly lose value and do not generate long-term income. Credit card debt, personal loans for discretionary expenses, and payday loans often fall into this category. Such debt carries high-interest rates, can quickly accumulate, and provides no return.

The Impact of Debt on Your Financial Planning:

Inhibits Savings and Investment: High levels of bad debt can eat into your monthly income, leaving less money for savings and investments. This can impede the growth of your retirement nest egg.

Interest Costs: Debt often comes with interest costs. The longer you take to pay off your debt, the more interest you'll end up paying, further draining your resources.

Credit Score: Mismanagement of debt can lead to missed or late payments, which can negatively impact your credit score. A poor credit score can affect your ability to secure loans in the future and can result in higher interest rates on borrowed money.

Managing Debt in Financial Planning:

Debt Payoff Strategy: Implement strategies like the debt snowball (paying off smallest debts first) or debt avalanche (paying off highest interest debts first) methods to reduce your debt load.

Consolidation and Refinancing: Consolidating multiple debts into one or refinancing existing debt to secure a lower interest rate can make debt management easier and less costly.

Budgeting: Regular budgeting can help ensure you live within your means and avoid unnecessary debt.

Debt and Retirement:

Entering retirement with significant debt can strain your fixed retirement income. As part of retirement planning, aim to pay off high-interest debts and consider the implications of carrying a mortgage or other debts into retirement.

Debt, when managed effectively, doesn't have to be a barrier to your financial goals. It's crucial to distinguish between good and bad debt, maintain a strategic approach towards debt reduction, and factor it into your overall financial planning and retirement strategy. In doing so, you ensure debt serves as a tool for building wealth, not an obstacle to your financial wellbeing.

Chapter 3: Establishing Retirement Goals

Identifying Personal and Financial Retirement Goals

Setting clear and specific retirement goals is the cornerstone of any retirement plan. Your goals shape your plan and serve as a roadmap to your desired future. They are a mix of your personal dreams and aspirations as well as financial targets that will enable you to live comfortably and sustainably in your golden years. Here are steps to help you identify your personal and financial retirement goals:

Visualizing Your Retirement Lifestyle:

Take time to imagine your retirement life in detail. What does a typical day look like? Are you traveling around the world, starting a business, dedicating yourself to a hobby, or spending quality time with family and friends? Do you see yourself relocating to a different city or even a different country? Your envisioned lifestyle will significantly influence your retirement expenses and thus your financial goals.

Estimating Your Retirement Expenses:

Once you have a vision for your retirement, the next step is to estimate the costs associated with that lifestyle. This includes everyday living expenses such as housing, food, utilities, and healthcare, as well as costs for your specific retirement goals like travel or philanthropy. It's also prudent to include potential expenses like long-term care or increased medical costs in your estimate.

Setting a Retirement Age:

Choosing when to retire will directly impact how much you need to save and how long those savings need to last. The earlier you retire, the more you need to save. Consider factors such as your health, job satisfaction, and Social Security benefits when deciding your retirement age.

Identifying Income Sources:

Your retirement income can come from multiple sources: Social Security, pension, retirement accounts like 401(k) or IRA, annuities, part-time work, rental income, etc. Identify these potential sources and estimate the monthly or annual income you can expect from each.

Determining Your Retirement Savings Goal:

With the estimated expenses, retirement age, and income sources in mind, you can determine how much you need to save for retirement. A common rule of thumb is to aim for a nest egg that is 25 times the amount of your first year of retirement expenses, after accounting for other guaranteed sources of income. Remember, this is a rough estimate; you might need more or less depending on your personal circumstances and market conditions.

Planning for the Unexpected:

Life is full of surprises, and it's important to factor in contingencies like medical emergencies or financial downturns. Having an emergency fund and adequate insurance coverage can provide a financial safety net in your retirement years.

Remember, retirement planning is not a one-time event but an ongoing process. Your goals may change over time as your circumstances evolve. Regularly reviewing and adjusting your goals ensures that your plan stays aligned with your vision of retirement, leading you towards a financially secure and fulfilling retired life.

Setting Realistic Expectations

Setting realistic expectations is an essential component of successful retirement planning. It involves striking a balance between your retirement dreams and what is financially feasible given your income, savings, investment returns, and life expectancy.

Understand Your Financial Capabilities:

It's essential to have a clear understanding of your financial capabilities. This includes your current income, savings, anticipated pension or social security benefits, investment returns, and potential inheritance. These factors will largely dictate the lifestyle you can afford in retirement.

Keep Inflation in Mind:

Inflation can erode your purchasing power over time. What seems like a substantial retirement fund now may not be enough 20 or 30 years down the line. When planning for retirement, consider the impact of inflation on your savings and the cost of living.

Consider Healthcare Costs:

Healthcare costs are a significant expense for many retirees and can be higher than anticipated. As you age, you may require more medical care, and costs for treatments and medications can add up. Consider these costs and potential long-term care when setting your retirement goals.

Be Cautious with Investment Returns:

It's crucial to be conservative when estimating future investment returns. While we all hope for high returns, it's safer to plan based on moderate or even low returns. Overestimating returns can leave you with a savings shortfall in retirement.

Factor in Longer Life Expectancy:

Thanks to advances in healthcare, people are living longer than ever before. This means your retirement savings may need to last for 20, 30, or even more years. Consider longevity risk when determining how much you need to save.

Be Flexible:

Life can throw curveballs, and the financial landscape can shift. It's vital to remain flexible with your retirement plans and be prepared to adjust your goals or strategies as necessary. Regular reviews of your retirement plan will allow you to adapt to changes and stay on track.

By setting realistic expectations, you can avoid common pitfalls and financial stress in your retirement years. It allows you to build a retirement plan that is robust, achievable, and aligned with your desired lifestyle. After all, your retirement should be a time of enjoyment and fulfillment, free from financial worry.

The Importance of Flexibility in Retirement Planning

Just as a ship's captain adjusts the course based on changing winds and tides, you must remain flexible in your retirement planning to navigate the unpredictable ebb and flow of life and financial markets. Having a flexible retirement plan is essential to managing risks and seizing opportunities that can affect your financial future.

Changing Personal Circumstances:

Life can surprise you with unexpected events like health issues, family responsibilities, or sudden unemployment. Alternatively, positive changes like an unexpected windfall or a higher-than-expected return on investments may also occur. A flexible retirement plan can adapt to these changes, ensuring that your financial security isn't compromised.

Market Fluctuations:

Financial markets can be volatile, and investment values can rise or fall significantly. If your retirement plan is rigid, a downturn in the market could seriously impact your retirement savings. Flexibility allows you to adjust your investment strategy based on market conditions, protecting your nest egg from major downturns and capitalizing on growth opportunities.

Inflation and Cost of Living:

Inflation can erode your purchasing power over time. Meanwhile, the cost of living may increase more than anticipated, particularly in areas like healthcare. Having the flexibility to adjust your retirement income or savings goals can help preserve your desired standard of living.

Legislative Changes:

Tax laws and retirement regulations can change, impacting your retirement savings and income. A flexible retirement plan allows for adjustments to take advantage of legislative changes or mitigate any negative impacts.

Longer Lifespan:

Thanks to advances in healthcare and healthier lifestyles, people are living longer. This increases the likelihood of outliving your savings if your retirement plan is too rigid. Flexibility in your plan allows you to adjust your savings goals, investment strategies, or retirement age to ensure your savings last as long as you do.

Flexibility in retirement planning means regularly reviewing and adjusting your plan based on changing circumstances and new information. It is about being proactive and prepared for change, rather than reactive and vulnerable. Ultimately, flexibility can enhance your financial resilience, helping ensure a comfortable and worry-free retirement, no matter what life throws your way.

Chapter 4: Strategies for Saving

Overview of Different Savings Strategies

Creating a substantial nest egg for retirement requires effective saving strategies. While the exact approach will depend on your unique circumstances, here are several common strategies that can assist in building your retirement savings:

Pay Yourself First:

One of the simplest and most effective strategies is to "pay yourself first." This means setting aside a portion of your income for savings before spending on anything else. Automating this process by setting up direct deposits into your savings or retirement account can make it effortless and ensure consistent savings.

Take Advantage of Employer Matching:

If your employer offers a retirement plan like a 401(k) with matching contributions, be sure to contribute at least enough to receive the full match. This is essentially free money and can significantly boost your retirement savings.

Maximize Tax-Advantaged Accounts:

Utilize tax-advantaged retirement accounts like 401(k)s, IRAs, and Health Savings Accounts (HSAs). These accounts offer tax deductions on contributions, tax-free growth, or tax-free withdrawals, depending on the type of account.

Utilize Catch-Up Contributions:

If you're age 50 or older, you're allowed to make additional catch-up contributions to your 401(k) and IRA. This can be a valuable strategy to boost your retirement savings as you approach retirement age.

Save Windfalls:

Extra money from a raise, bonus, tax refund, or inheritance provides an opportunity to bolster your savings. While it's tempting to spend windfalls, putting at least a portion towards your retirement can have a significant long-term impact.

Gradually Increase Savings Rate:

Increasing your savings rate over time can also help build your nest egg. This could be as simple as increasing your 401(k) contribution by 1% each year or putting a portion of each salary increase towards savings.

Diversified Investment Strategy:

A diversified investment strategy can help grow your savings and mitigate risk. This involves spreading your investments across different asset classes like stocks, bonds, and real estate. A financial advisor or robo-advisor can assist in building a diversified investment portfolio based on your risk tolerance and retirement goals.

Delay Social Security:

If you can afford to do so, delaying Social Security benefits until after your full retirement age can increase your monthly benefit, providing more retirement income in the long run.

By using a combination of these strategies, you can grow your retirement savings and create a financial cushion for your golden years. It's important to review your savings strategies regularly and adjust as needed based on your financial situation and retirement goals. Remember, every bit saved today brings you one step closer to a secure and comfortable retirement.

The Power of Compound Interest

Compound interest is one of the most powerful tools at your disposal when saving for retirement. Often referred to as 'earning interest on your interest,' compound interest can significantly magnify the growth of your savings over time, turning even small regular contributions into a substantial sum.

Understanding Compound Interest:

Compound interest is the process by which the interest earned on your savings or investments is added back to the original amount, which then itself earns interest. This creates a snowball effect, where the total amount of interest earned accelerates over time as it's continually reinvested. The longer your money is invested, the more time it has to compound, and the greater the impact on your total savings.

The Magic of Compounding:

To illustrate the power of compound interest, consider a $10,000 investment earning a 7% annual return. Without compounding, a simple 7% interest would yield $700 per year, amounting to $7,000 after 10 years. However, with annual compounding, you would earn not just 7% on the initial $10,000 but also 7% on the interest accumulated each year. This would result in a total of over $19,600 after 10 years - almost double the initial investment.

The Importance of Time:

The most crucial element in compounding is time. The longer your money is invested, the more compounding cycles it goes through, and the larger your investment grows. Starting to save and invest early in your career takes maximum advantage of compound interest and can lead to significantly more substantial growth than if you start later, even if you save more in the later years.

Regular Contributions:

Making regular contributions to your retirement savings enhances the power of compound interest. Even small amounts can grow substantially over time due to compounding. This principle underlines the importance of consistent saving, even if you can only afford to set aside a small amount regularly.

The Effect of Compounding Frequency:

The frequency of compounding can also have a significant impact on your savings. Interest can be compounded on various schedules: annually, semi-annually, quarterly, monthly, or even daily. Generally, the more frequently interest is compounded, the greater the overall return.

In conclusion, compound interest can be your best friend when saving for retirement. It rewards patience and consistency, turning your retirement savings into a powerful engine of growth. As Albert Einstein famously said, "Compound interest is the eighth wonder of the world. He who understands it, earns it; he who doesn't, pays it."

Balancing Saving with Living Expenses and Debt Repayment

Balancing the act of saving for retirement, managing living expenses, and repaying debt can seem like a daunting task. However, with a thoughtful strategy, it's possible to maintain this delicate financial balance without sacrificing your lifestyle or financial well-being. Here's how:

Establish a Budget:

A budget is a blueprint of your income and expenses. It allows you to see where your money is going, identify necessary and discretionary spending, and determine how much you can realistically put towards saving and debt repayment. Start by listing all your income sources and expenses, then allocate funds to savings, debt repayment, and living costs.

Prioritize High-Interest Debt:

While saving for retirement is crucial, high-interest debt can erode your financial stability and offset any gains you may earn from investments. Therefore, it's often wise to prioritize paying off high-interest debt, like credit card debt, before ramping up retirement savings.

Emergency Fund:

Before focusing on retirement savings or aggressive debt repayment, it's important to establish an emergency fund. This fund is meant to cover unexpected expenses like car repairs, medical bills, or job loss, preventing you from dipping into retirement savings or taking on more debt.

Make Use of Employer Retirement Match:

Even when paying down debt, try to contribute enough to your employer-sponsored retirement plan to get the full employer match, if available. It's essentially free money and a guaranteed return on your investment.

Automate Savings:

Automating contributions to your retirement savings can ensure consistency and help resist the temptation to skip or reduce contributions when money is tight.

Manage Living Expenses:

Look for ways to reduce unnecessary expenses in your budget. This could involve cutting back on dining out, downsizing your housing, or negotiating lower rates on utilities or insurance. Savings can be redirected towards retirement savings or paying down debt.

Create Additional Income Streams:

If possible, consider creating additional income streams. This could be through a side job, freelancing, or renting out a room in your home. Extra income can help boost savings and expedite debt repayment.

Balancing saving, living expenses, and debt repayment is a juggling act, but it is achievable with discipline and careful planning. And remember, financial plans can and should be adjusted as your circumstances change over time. Your future retired self will thank you for the efforts you make today.

Chapter 5: Introduction to Investing

Basic Principles of Investing

Investing is an integral part of retirement planning, as it allows your money to grow over time, helping you accumulate a larger nest egg for your retirement years. Whether you're a seasoned investor or a beginner, understanding and applying the basic principles of investing is key to successful wealth accumulation. Here are some foundational concepts:

Risk and Return:

Investing always involves some level of risk. Generally, investments with the potential for higher returns also come with higher risk. This fundamental relationship is called the risk-return tradeoff. The key is to find a balance that suits your risk tolerance and financial goals.

Diversification:

"Diversification" refers to spreading your investments across various asset classes such as stocks, bonds, real estate, and cash equivalents to reduce risk. It's often said, "Don't put all your eggs in one basket," and this rings true in investing. By diversifying, you can help cushion your portfolio against volatility in any one investment.

Asset Allocation:

Asset allocation is the process of dividing your investment portfolio among different asset classes. Your ideal asset allocation will depend on your financial goals, risk tolerance, and investment timeline. A proper asset allocation strategy can help you manage risk while maximizing returns.

Compound Interest:

Compound interest plays a significant role in the growth of your investments. It refers to earning interest on your initial investment and the accumulated interest over time. The power of compounding increases with time, highlighting the importance of starting to invest as early as possible.

Dollar-Cost Averaging:

Dollar-cost averaging involves investing a fixed amount of money at regular intervals, regardless of market conditions. This approach can mitigate the impact of market volatility and reduce the risk of making a large investment at an inopportune time.

Patience and Long-Term Investing:

Investing for retirement is a long-term game. Market fluctuations can be stressful in the short term, but historically, markets have trended upwards over the long term. Patience and staying the course, rather than trying to time the market, can lead to better investment outcomes.

Regular Review and Rebalancing:

Investing is not a set-it-and-forget-it activity. Regularly reviewing your portfolio to assess performance and rebalancing to maintain your desired asset allocation are important tasks. Changes in market conditions, personal circumstances, or financial goals may necessitate adjustments to your investment strategy.

By understanding and applying these basic principles, you can navigate the investing journey with more confidence and clarity. Remember, investing for retirement is not about getting rich quick but growing your wealth steadily and sustainably over time.

Risk and Return

The concepts of risk and return are at the very heart of investing. Understanding this relationship is essential for making informed investment decisions that align with your retirement goals and risk tolerance.

What is Risk?

In the context of investing, risk refers to the potential for your investments to lose value. It is the uncertainty related to the return of your investment. All investments carry some level of risk, stemming from various factors like market volatility, inflation, interest rates, or specific issues related to a particular company or sector.

What is Return?

Return, on the other hand, is the gain or loss made on an investment over a specific period. It is usually expressed as a percentage of the investment's initial cost. Returns can come from capital gains (selling an investment for more than you paid for it) or income (such as dividends or interest).

The Risk-Return Tradeoff:

The risk-return tradeoff is a fundamental concept in investing that suggests that potential returns rise with an increase in risk. Low levels of uncertainty (low-risk investments) are associated with low potential returns, whereas high levels of uncertainty (high-risk investments) are associated with high potential returns.

For instance, a U.S. Treasury bond is considered one of the safest investments and thus offers a relatively low return. Conversely, investing in a startup company's stock is riskier, as the company may either fail or succeed. Thus, while the potential for loss is greater, the potential returns are also significantly higher.

Risk Tolerance:

Risk tolerance is a personal measure of the degree of uncertainty an investor can handle regarding a negative change in the value of their portfolio. It varies from person to person. Factors influencing risk tolerance include financial goals, timeline (how soon you'll need the money), income stability, and personal comfort with uncertainty.

Managing Risk and Return:

Balancing risk and return in a portfolio is a fundamental aspect of investment strategy. Depending on your risk tolerance and investment goals, you may choose a conservative portfolio (lower risk, lower return), a moderate portfolio (medium risk, medium return), or an aggressive portfolio (high risk, high return).

Diversification is a key strategy to manage the risk-return tradeoff. By spreading investments across various asset types and sectors, you can protect your portfolio from significant losses while still pursuing returns. Regularly reviewing and rebalancing your portfolio can also help manage risk and align your investments with your financial goals.

In conclusion, understanding the relationship between risk and return is crucial for effective investment management. It can help you construct a portfolio that suits your risk tolerance and maximizes potential returns for your level of accepted risk, bringing you closer to your retirement goals.

Diversification and Asset Allocation

Diversification and asset allocation are two interconnected strategies used in investing to manage risk and optimize returns. They are crucial components of a sound retirement planning strategy.

Diversification:

Diversification involves spreading your investments across various asset classes and within those classes to reduce the risk associated with putting all your money in a single investment or type of investment. The principle behind diversification is that different types of investments will perform differently at different times.

For example, if you diversify your portfolio by investing in stocks across a range of sectors, a decline in one sector, such as technology, may be offset by an uptick in another, like healthcare. This strategy can help smooth out the volatility in your portfolio's overall performance, limiting potential losses without necessarily sacrificing returns.

Asset Allocation:

Asset allocation takes diversification a step further by helping you determine what proportion of your portfolio to devote to different asset classes, such as equities, bonds, and cash equivalents.

Your asset allocation should align with your financial goals, risk tolerance, and investment timeline. For example, younger investors with a higher risk tolerance and longer investment timeline might lean heavily towards equities, which tend to offer higher returns but also higher volatility. On the other hand, individuals nearing retirement may favor bonds, which offer lower returns but more stability.

Implementing Diversification and Asset Allocation:

Implementing these strategies typically involves a mix of different types of assets. For example:

- **Equities**: These are shares in a company. They tend to be riskier but offer higher potential returns.
- **Bonds**: These are essentially loans to a government or company. They tend to be safer but offer lower potential returns.
- **Cash** Equivalents: These are safe, liquid investments such as money market funds. They offer stability and are useful for preserving capital or providing income in retirement.
- **Real Estate**: This includes physical property or real estate investment trusts (REITs). Real estate can provide both income and capital appreciation.
- **Commodities**: These include physical assets like gold, oil, and agricultural products. They can act as a hedge against inflation.

Regular Rebalancing:

Once you've established an asset allocation, it's important to periodically rebalance your portfolio. Over time, some investments will grow faster than others, which may throw your portfolio off balance. By rebalancing, you can ensure your portfolio remains aligned with your target allocation and risk level.

Diversification and asset allocation are not one-time tasks but ongoing processes that evolve with your changing financial needs, market conditions, and life events. Both strategies play a crucial role in creating a robust investment portfolio that can help you achieve your retirement goals while managing risk.

Chapter 6: Investing for Retirement

Overview of Retirement-Specific Investment Options

When investing for retirement, you have a variety of account options available, each with unique features, advantages, and limitations. Understanding these can help you determine the best approach for your retirement savings. Here are some of the most common retirement-specific investment options:

401(k) Plans:

A 401(k) is a retirement savings plan sponsored by an employer. It lets employees save and invest a portion of their paycheck before taxes are taken out. Taxes aren't paid until the money is withdrawn from the account. Many employers offer to match a portion of your contributions, which can significantly enhance the growth of your savings.

Traditional Individual Retirement Accounts (IRAs):

A traditional IRA is a tax-deferred retirement savings account. You pay taxes on your money only when you make withdrawals in retirement. Contributions to a traditional IRA may be tax-deductible, depending on your income and whether you or your spouse have a workplace retirement plan.

Roth IRAs:

Unlike a traditional IRA, Roth IRA contributions are made with after-tax dollars. This means you pay taxes now, but withdrawals in retirement, including earnings, are tax-free, provided certain conditions are met. Roth IRAs can be particularly beneficial if you expect to be in a higher tax bracket in retirement than you are now.

Roth 401(k) Plans:

A Roth 401(k) combines features of the 401(k) and the Roth IRA. It's offered by employers like a regular 401(k), but as with a Roth IRA, contributions are made with after-tax dollars. While there's no tax break on contributions, money can be withdrawn tax-free in retirement, provided certain conditions are met.

SIMPLE IRAs:

Savings Incentive Match Plan for Employees (SIMPLE) IRAs are available to small businesses with 100 or fewer employees. They work similarly to a traditional IRA but have higher contribution limits. Employers must either match employee contributions or make unmatched contributions.

SEP IRAs:

A Simplified Employee Pension (SEP) IRA is designed for self-employed people and small-business owners. They work similarly to traditional IRAs but allow for higher contributions.

Health Savings Accounts (HSAs):

While primarily designed to help individuals save for medical costs on a tax-free basis, HSAs have potential as a retirement savings tool due to their triple-tax advantages: contributions are tax-deductible, the money grows tax-free, and withdrawals for qualified medical expenses are also tax-free.

Each of these investment options has rules concerning eligibility, contribution limits, tax treatment, and withdrawal requirements. It's important to understand these aspects and consider seeking advice from a financial advisor or tax professional to choose the most suitable options for your personal circumstances and retirement goals.

When to Start Investing for Retirement

Determining when to start investing for retirement is a question that most individuals grapple with at some point in their lives. The simple answer is: as soon as you can. Here's why:

The Power of Compounding:

One of the most compelling reasons to start investing early is to take advantage of the power of compounding. This refers to earning returns not just on your original investment, but also on the returns that investment has already generated. The longer your money is invested, the more time it has to grow, and the greater the power of compounding becomes.

Time to Recover from Market Downturns:

Investing sooner rather than later also gives your portfolio more time to recover from market downturns. While markets can be volatile in the short term, they have historically trended upwards in the long term. Starting early allows you to ride out these inevitable downturns and still come out ahead.

Financial Habits:

Starting to invest early encourages good financial habits. It instills a discipline of regular saving and investing, making it a routine part of your life rather than a task to be postponed.

Higher Risk Tolerance:

Younger investors generally have a higher risk tolerance, as they have more time to recover from any potential losses. This means they can afford to invest more heavily in higher-risk, higher-return assets, such as stocks, which can lead to greater wealth accumulation over time.

Achievement of Retirement Goals:

The earlier you start investing, the more likely you are to reach your retirement goals. If you delay investing until later in life, you may need to contribute significantly more to achieve the same retirement nest egg or accept a lower standard of living in retirement.

Even if you're starting late, remember that it's never too late to invest for retirement. Any amount you can invest now provides a greater chance of a secure and comfortable retirement than not investing at all.

In conclusion, the best time to start investing for retirement is as soon as you start earning income. The next best time is now.

Balancing Risk and Return as Retirement Approaches

As you approach retirement, your investment strategy should shift to prioritize preserving your accumulated savings while still aiming for a degree of growth. Balancing risk and return during this critical period requires careful planning and a nuanced approach.

Lowering Risk Exposure:

In general, as retirement nears, the proportion of higher-risk investments such as equities (stocks) in your portfolio should decrease. This is because you have less time to recover from potential market downturns. Consequently, you should progressively shift towards lower-risk, stable investments like bonds and cash equivalents.

Maintaining Some Growth Potential:

While it's important to preserve capital as you approach retirement, it's equally critical to ensure your investments continue to grow. Given the potential for a retirement period of 20 years or more, retaining some exposure to equities can help your retirement savings keep pace with inflation and increase your likelihood of not outliving your assets.

Reassessing Asset Allocation:

Your asset allocation should evolve as you get closer to retirement. This involves rebalancing your portfolio to reflect your changing risk tolerance and financial goals. Regularly reviewing and adjusting your asset allocation helps to ensure it remains aligned with your retirement objectives.

Considering Annuities:

Annuities can provide a steady income stream in retirement, much like a pension. You pay a lump sum or series of payments to an insurance company, which in turn provides regular payments to you, either immediately or at a specified future date. While annuities can provide stability, they are complex financial products with various pros and cons. Therefore, careful consideration and possibly professional advice should be sought before incorporating annuities into your retirement strategy.

Seeking Professional Advice:

As retirement approaches, the financial decisions you make can have lasting impacts. A financial advisor can provide personalized advice based on your unique situation. They can help you navigate the complexities of retirement planning, including the task of balancing risk and return as retirement nears.

Remember, moving towards retirement doesn't mean eliminating all risk from your portfolio. Instead, it's about finding the right balance between risk and return that allows for potential growth while still protecting the wealth you've accumulated throughout your working life.

Chapter 7: Understanding Social Security and Pensions

How Social Security and Pensions Work

Social Security and pensions represent significant sources of income for many retirees. Understanding how these systems work can help you plan more effectively for your retirement.

Social Security:

Social Security is a federal program in the United States that provides benefits to retirees, as well as to disabled individuals and to families in which a spouse or parent dies. The program is funded through payroll taxes.

Your Social Security retirement benefits are based on your earnings over your working life. The Social Security Administration uses a formula to calculate your primary insurance amount (PIA), which is the monthly benefit you're entitled to receive at your full retirement age (FRA). The FRA varies depending on your year of birth, ranging from 65 for those born before 1938 to 67 for those born in 1960 or later.

You can choose to start receiving Social Security benefits as early as age 62, but your benefits will be reduced if you do. Conversely, if you delay taking Social Security beyond your FRA, your benefits will increase until age 70.

Pensions:

A pension is a type of retirement plan where an employer promises to pay a specified monthly amount to employees upon their retirement. This is in contrast to defined contribution plans like a 401(k), where the amount of money the employee has at retirement depends on the contributions made and the performance of the investments.

The amount of pension income you'll receive generally depends on factors like your years of service, your salary, and the specifics of the pension plan. Some pensions offer cost-of-living adjustments (COLAs) that raise the benefits over time to keep pace with inflation.

Pensions are less common today than they used to be, with many employers moving to defined contribution plans. If you're lucky enough to have a pension, it can provide a stable base of retirement income.

It's important to note that while Social Security and pensions can provide substantial retirement income, they're not likely to be enough on their own to maintain your pre-retirement standard of living. Most financial advisors suggest that these sources should be supplemented with personal savings and investments.

Finally, always keep abreast of changes in these programs, as legislative and regulatory modifications can impact benefit levels and eligibility rules. Understanding how Social Security and pensions work can aid you in making informed decisions for a financially secure retirement.

Maximizing Social Security Benefits

Social Security represents a crucial income source for many retirees, so understanding how to maximize these benefits can significantly enhance your financial security in retirement. Here are a few strategies to consider:

Delay Taking Benefits:

The simplest and most effective way to maximize your Social Security benefit is by delaying the start of your benefits until after your full retirement age (FRA). For every year you delay, up until age 70, your monthly benefit will increase by a certain percentage. The specific increase varies depending on your birth year, but it ranges from 5.5% to 8% per year. By waiting until age 70 to begin taking Social Security, you can significantly boost your monthly benefit amount.

Consider Your Spousal Benefits:

If you're married, divorced, or widowed, you may have the option of claiming Social Security benefits based on your own work record or your spouse's (or ex-spouse's). The spousal benefit can be as much as 50% of the higher-earning spouse's benefit at FRA.

Understanding these rules can help you decide when and how to claim to maximize your total benefits.

Keep Working:

Social Security calculates your benefits based on your 35 highest-earning years. If you didn't work a full 35 years, the calculation will include zeros, which can significantly lower your benefit. Therefore, working longer, even if it's part-time, can boost your benefits by replacing zero-earning years or lower-earning years with higher-earning years.

Minimize Taxes:

Up to 85% of your Social Security benefits may be taxable, depending on your combined income (your adjusted gross income + non-taxable interest + 50% of your Social Security benefits). Understanding these rules can help you take steps to minimize the tax you pay on your benefits, such as by strategically drawing down retirement accounts.

Consider Professional Advice:

Social Security rules are complex, and the best claiming strategy depends on numerous factors, including your health, life expectancy, need for income, and whether or not you're married. Therefore, it can be beneficial to consult with a financial advisor or other professional who is well-versed in Social Security rules and strategies.

Maximizing Social Security benefits is a critical aspect of retirement planning. By understanding the system's rules and considering your personal circumstances, you can make informed decisions that optimize your retirement income.

The Current State of Pension Systems Worldwide

Pension systems are an integral part of retirement planning worldwide, providing a source of income to individuals in their post-working years. However, the state of pension systems varies dramatically from country to country, reflecting different societal norms, economic conditions, and government policies. As of the mid-2020s, here are some general trends observed:

Transition from Defined Benefit to Defined Contribution:

Similar to the United States, many countries are experiencing a shift from defined benefit (DB) schemes, where employees receive a guaranteed income in retirement, to defined contribution (DC) schemes, where retirement income is dependent on investment returns. This transition transfers the investment risk from the employer to the employee, emphasizing the importance of individual financial planning and investment management skills.

Aging Populations:

Globally, populations are aging, and the proportion of individuals in retirement compared to those in the workforce is increasing. This demographic shift places significant pressure on state-funded pension systems, which are often funded by current workers. Countries such as Japan, Germany, and Italy are facing serious challenges to maintain their pension systems in light of these demographic changes.

Pension System Reforms:

In response to these pressures, many countries are undergoing pension system reforms. These include increasing the retirement age, changing benefit calculations, encouraging private savings, and introducing automatic enrollment in pension schemes.

Variance in Pension Adequacy:

Pension adequacy, or the extent to which pension income allows individuals to maintain a reasonable living standard in retirement, varies widely. Some countries, like the Netherlands and Denmark, are renowned for their robust pension systems. In contrast, other countries are grappling with pension poverty, where the income provided by pensions is insufficient, leading to economic hardship among retirees.

Impact of Economic Conditions:

The state of the global economy and investment markets significantly impacts pension systems, particularly defined contribution plans. The events of the last decade, including economic crises and the COVID-19 pandemic, have brought to light the vulnerabilities of relying solely on market-dependent pension systems.

In conclusion, while pension systems remain a key component of retirement income worldwide, they are undergoing significant changes. Understanding these global trends can provide insights into the future of retirement and inform personal retirement planning strategies.

Chapter 8: Healthcare and Insurance in Retirement

Projecting Healthcare Costs in Retirement

Healthcare can represent one of the most significant expenses in retirement, and costs can be challenging to predict due to factors such as personal health status, the rate of healthcare inflation, and policy changes in public healthcare programs. Nevertheless, having a strategy to estimate these expenses is crucial for a sound retirement plan.

Average Healthcare Costs in Retirement:

As a starting point, consider what the average retiree spends on healthcare. According to the Center for Retirement Research at Boston College, an average retired couple at age 65 can expect to spend around $300,000 on healthcare throughout their retirement, not including long-term care like nursing home expenses. Keep in mind, though, that these figures are averages and can vary greatly based on individual circumstances.

Medicare Coverage and Costs:

In the U.S., most individuals become eligible for Medicare at age 65. While Medicare covers a significant portion of healthcare costs, it doesn't cover everything. Out-of-pocket costs including premiums, copayments, deductibles, and services not covered by Medicare (like most dental care, eye exams related to prescriptions glasses, and hearing aids) can add up. Additionally, prescription drug costs can be high even with Medicare Part D coverage. Researching Medicare's coverage gaps will help you estimate potential out-of-pocket costs.

Personal Health and Family History:

Your personal health status and family health history are important factors to consider when projecting healthcare costs. Chronic or serious illnesses can result in significantly higher healthcare costs in retirement. It might be beneficial to discuss potential future healthcare needs with your doctor.

Long-Term Care:

The U.S. Department of Health and Human Services estimates that 70% of those turning 65 will need some form of long-term care in their lifetime. However, such care can be incredibly expensive and is not fully covered by Medicare. Consideration should be given to how you will pay for long-term care if it becomes necessary, whether through long-term care insurance, self-insurance, or other means.

Inflation:

Healthcare costs have historically risen faster than general inflation. When projecting healthcare costs in retirement, it's important to factor in an appropriate rate of healthcare inflation.

Given the uncertainty of healthcare costs, it may be beneficial to take a conservative approach, overestimating rather than underestimating these expenses. A health savings account (HSA) or other dedicated healthcare fund can be beneficial in preparing for these inevitable costs. Consulting with a financial advisor or healthcare consultant can also provide personalized projections based on your unique circumstances.

Understanding Medicare and Other Healthcare Options

Healthcare coverage is a critical part of retirement planning. In the United States, most people become eligible for Medicare at age 65, but there are other options and supplemental plans to consider as well. Let's delve into these options:

Medicare:

Medicare is a federal health insurance program primarily for individuals aged 65 and older, but it also covers some younger people with certain disabilities. Medicare has four parts:

- Part A covers hospital stays, skilled nursing facility care, hospice care, and some home health care.

- Part B covers certain doctors' services, outpatient care, medical supplies, and preventive services.

- Part C, also known as Medicare Advantage, is an alternative to traditional Medicare (Parts A and B) that's offered by private insurance companies. These plans often include prescription drug coverage and may include additional benefits not covered by traditional Medicare.

- Part D adds prescription drug coverage to original Medicare, some Medicare Cost Plans, some Medicare Private-Fee-for-Service Plans, and Medicare Medical Savings Account Plans.

While Medicare provides comprehensive health coverage, it doesn't cover everything. Some services, such as most dental care, long-term care, eye exams related to prescription glasses, and hearing aids, are not covered.

Medigap:

Medigap, also known as Medicare Supplement Insurance, is private insurance that helps cover some of the healthcare costs that Medicare doesn't, like copayments, coinsurance, and deductibles. Some Medigap policies also offer coverage for services that Medicare doesn't, like medical care when you travel outside the U.S. It's important to note that Medigap policies generally don't cover long-term care, vision or dental care, hearing aids, eyeglasses, or private-duty nursing.

Medicaid:

Medicaid is a state and federal program that provides health coverage for some low-income people, families and children, pregnant women, the elderly, and people with disabilities. Medicaid programs must follow federal guidelines, but they vary somewhat from state to state.

Long-Term Care Insurance:

As mentioned earlier, Medicare and most health insurance plans, including Medigap, don't cover long-term custodial care, which is assistance with daily living activities like bathing, dressing, and eating. Long-term care insurance can help cover the cost of these services if you're unable to perform them yourself due to a chronic illness, disability, or other condition.

Health Savings Account (HSA) or Flexible Spending Account (FSA):

These are accounts in which you can contribute pre-tax dollars to pay for eligible healthcare expenses. An HSA is often paired with a high-deductible health plan (HDHP), and unlike an FSA, an HSA allows you to roll over the money from year to year and to invest the funds.

Understanding your healthcare options can help you make an informed decision that suits your needs and financial situation. It's always beneficial to consult with a healthcare advisor or financial planner to discuss your personal circumstances and guide you through the decision-making process.

The Role of Insurance in Retirement Planning

Insurance, in various forms, plays a pivotal role in retirement planning. It can provide financial protection against unforeseen health expenses, the need for long-term care, the death of a spouse, and even outliving one's savings. Let's explore some key insurance types that are relevant to retirement planning:

Health Insurance:

As previously discussed, Medicare serves as the cornerstone of healthcare coverage for most retirees, but it doesn't cover everything. Medigap policies, Medicare Advantage plans, and other supplemental insurance can help fill the gaps. Adequate health insurance coverage can prevent high medical expenses from depleting retirement savings.

Long-Term Care Insurance:

Long-term care insurance can provide coverage for care not covered by Medicare, such as home care, assisted living, or nursing home care, in the event you are unable to perform certain activities of daily living. This type of insurance can be costly but can also protect substantial retirement assets if such care is needed.

Life Insurance:

If you have dependents who rely on your income, life insurance can provide them with financial protection in the event of your death. Some retirees may no longer need life insurance if they have enough savings or if their dependents are financially independent. However, others may use life insurance as a tool for estate planning or leaving a financial legacy.

Homeowners/Renters Insurance:

For many individuals, a home represents one of the most significant investments they've made. Homeowners insurance can protect this asset from damages caused by things like fire or theft. Similarly, renters insurance can protect the value of personal belongings in a rented property.

Auto Insurance:

Auto insurance is required by law in most states, and it's important to maintain appropriate coverage in retirement. Some retirees may find their insurance needs change in retirement if they no longer commute to work daily.

Annuities:

Though not traditionally thought of as "insurance," annuities can play a similar role by providing a guaranteed income stream for a set period or for life, essentially insuring against the risk of outliving one's savings. Annuities can be complex and may not be suitable for everyone, so it's essential to understand the terms and costs associated with them.

In summary, while the specific insurance needs will vary depending on personal circumstances, insurance plays a crucial role in protecting against a variety of risks in retirement. A comprehensive retirement plan often includes several types of insurance coverage, providing a safety net that allows retirees to enjoy their golden years without constant worry about financial ruin from unexpected events. As always, it's wise to consult with a financial planner or insurance professional when determining your insurance needs for retirement.

Chapter 9: Real Estate and Retirement

The Role of Home Ownership in Retirement Planning

Homeownership is often one of the largest components of an individual's net worth and therefore plays a crucial role in retirement planning. It's not just a place to live; it's also a significant financial asset that can affect your financial security, lifestyle, and even the timing of your retirement. Here's how:

A Source of Stability:

Owning your home provides a measure of stability in retirement. Unlike renters, homeowners who have paid off their mortgages have the assurance of a place to live, without the worry of rising rental costs. This can make budgeting easier since housing costs often represent a substantial portion of living expenses.

Equity and Wealth:

The equity in your home (the home's value minus any remaining mortgage balance) represents a form of wealth that can be tapped in retirement if needed. You can access this equity through selling the house, a home equity loan, or a reverse mortgage.

Downsizing or Relocating:

Retirement is a time when many people consider downsizing to a smaller home or relocating to a different area, perhaps closer to family or in a region with a lower cost of living or more desirable climate. Both downsizing and relocating can potentially free up home equity that can be used to support your retirement lifestyle.

Rental Income:

If you have extra space in your home, such as a basement or a separate unit, you might be able to rent it out for additional income in retirement. Alternatively, if you own a second home, you could consider renting it out, either to long-term tenants or as a vacation rental.

Estate Planning:

For many people, their home is not just a financial asset, but also a part of their legacy they wish to leave to their children or other heirs. This desire can influence decisions about whether to sell the home, take out a reverse mortgage, or how to handle the home in the estate planning process.

Taxes:

In many jurisdictions, homeownership comes with tax benefits that can be especially valuable in retirement. These may include deductions for mortgage interest or property taxes, or the ability to exclude some or all of the gain from the sale of the home from taxable income.

In conclusion, homeownership plays a multifaceted role in retirement planning, providing not only a place to live but also potential sources of income, financial stability, and tax benefits. As with other aspects of retirement planning, decisions about homeownership should be made in the context of your overall financial situation, personal preferences, and retirement goals. Consulting with a financial advisor or real estate professional can provide valuable guidance.

Downsizing, Reverse Mortgages, and Other Real Estate Strategies

Navigating the world of real estate during retirement can present a host of opportunities. From downsizing to reverse mortgages, there are several strategies available that can provide financial benefits. Here's a deeper dive into these strategies:

Downsizing:

Downsizing involves selling your current home and moving into a smaller, less expensive one. The equity from your original home can be used to purchase the new one (possibly without a mortgage), with the surplus going into your retirement savings. Downsizing can also decrease costs associated with home maintenance, taxes, and utilities.

Reverse Mortgages:

A reverse mortgage allows homeowners age 62 or older to convert part of the equity in their homes into cash. Unlike a traditional home equity loan or second mortgage, no repayment is required until the borrower(s) no longer use the home as their primary residence. It's an option that can provide additional income during retirement but should be considered carefully due to the high fees involved and the impact on estate planning.

Renting Out Property:

If you have extra space or a second property, you might consider renting it out for additional income. This can be a short-term vacation rental or a long-term residential lease. Before you decide, make sure to consider the potential tax implications, maintenance and repair costs, and the demands of being a landlord.

Relocating:

Moving to a more affordable area or a state with lower taxes can reduce living expenses and stretch retirement savings. Some may choose to live overseas in a country with a lower cost of living. This is a major decision that will impact not just finances, but lifestyle and proximity to family and friends, so thorough research and planning are essential.

Home Equity Loan or Line of Credit:

If you need cash but don't want to move or sell your home, a home equity loan or a home equity line of credit (HELOC) might be options to consider. These allow you to borrow against the equity in your home, but they require you to repay the borrowed amount with interest, unlike a reverse mortgage.

Sale-Leaseback:

In a sale-leaseback arrangement, you sell your home and then lease it back from the new owner. This allows you to access the equity in your home while continuing to live in it. However, this strategy does have risks, including the potential for increased rent in the future.

Each of these strategies has potential benefits and drawbacks, and not every strategy is right for everyone. It's important to understand the implications of each option and consider how they align with your overall retirement goals. Consulting with a financial advisor or a real estate professional can provide valuable insights tailored to your personal circumstances.

Renting vs. Owning in Retirement

The choice between renting and owning in retirement is a significant decision that can greatly impact your financial situation and quality of life. There's no one-size-fits-all answer, as the best choice depends on your individual circumstances, preferences, and goals. Let's discuss some of the key considerations:

Renting in Retirement:

Renting can offer several advantages during your retirement years:

Flexibility: Renting offers the opportunity to live in different locations, whether you desire to be closer to family or simply want a change of scenery.

Less Maintenance: As a tenant, you're not typically responsible for the maintenance and upkeep of the property. This can lead to fewer headaches and more time to enjoy retirement.

Liquidity: If the majority of your net worth is tied up in your home, selling your property and renting can free up a significant amount of capital that can be used for living expenses, healthcare, travel, or other pursuits in retirement.

However, there are also potential drawbacks to renting:

Lack of Equity: When you rent, your housing costs won't allow you to build equity. You're essentially paying for a service (housing) and will own no property at the end of your lease.

Rising Costs: Rent may increase over time due to inflation or changes in the rental market.

Owning in Retirement:

Homeownership can also have benefits:

Stability: Owning a home can provide a sense of stability and predictability. If your mortgage is paid off, you'll have the security of a place to live without worrying about future rent increases.

Equity: Your home could increase in value over time, which might allow you to leave a larger estate to your heirs or tap into the home's equity if needed.

Tax Benefits: In some jurisdictions, homeowners may be eligible for tax benefits such as deductions for mortgage interest or property taxes, or the ability to exclude some or all of the gain from the sale of the home from taxable income.

Drawbacks of homeownership include:

Maintenance and Unexpected Repairs: Homeownership comes with ongoing costs like property taxes, insurance, and maintenance. Large, unexpected repairs can also occur, which can be particularly stressful if you're on a fixed income.

Less Liquidity: Home equity is not easily accessible in a pinch and selling a house can be a lengthy process.

In conclusion, there are compelling reasons for both renting and owning in retirement, and the best decision depends on your personal circumstances and financial situation. A financial advisor can provide personalized advice based on your retirement goals and lifestyle preferences.

Chapter 10: Tax Planning for Retirement

Tax Implications of Retirement Income

Understanding the tax implications of various sources of retirement income is key to maximizing your wealth and minimizing your tax liability. The tax rules that apply to each can significantly affect how much income you'll actually have available to spend in retirement. Here are some major sources of retirement income and their associated tax implications:

Social Security Benefits:

In the United States, depending on your income level and filing status, up to 85% of your Social Security benefits may be subject to federal income tax. Some states also tax Social Security benefits, while others do not.

Pensions:

Traditional pensions are usually taxable. The amount of tax you'll pay depends on your overall income, deductions, tax credits, and the tax brackets for the year.

Retirement Account Withdrawals:

Withdrawals from tax-deferred retirement accounts, such as traditional 401(k)s and IRAs, are generally taxed as ordinary income. Roth 401(k)s and Roth IRAs, on the other hand, offer tax-free withdrawals in retirement, assuming you meet certain conditions.

Investment Income:

Income from investments held outside of retirement accounts can also be subject to tax. The tax rate depends on the type of investment income:

- Interest income is typically taxed as ordinary income.
- Dividend income may qualify for lower capital gains tax rates.
- Capital gains from selling investments can be taxed at lower long-term capital gains rates if you held the investments for over a year before selling. Short-term capital gains are generally taxed at your ordinary income tax rate.

Annuities:

The tax treatment of annuity income depends on the type of annuity and how it was funded. Payments from a qualified annuity, such as one purchased with pre-tax dollars within a retirement account, are generally taxable. Payments from a non-qualified annuity (purchased with after-tax dollars) are partially taxable. The portion of each payment that represents a return of your initial investment is tax-free, while any earnings are taxable.

76

Real Estate Income:

If you rent out property, the rental income you receive is generally taxable. However, you can offset this income with expenses like depreciation, property taxes, mortgage interest, insurance, repairs, and maintenance.

Part-time or Gig Work:

If you continue to work in retirement, whether part-time or as a freelancer, the income you earn is subject to income tax and may also impact the taxation of your Social Security benefits.

Being aware of the tax implications of these sources of income can inform your retirement planning strategies. You may wish to consider strategies such as income bunching, tax-efficient withdrawal strategies, or tax-efficient investment strategies to minimize your overall tax liability. As tax laws are complex and change frequently, it's a good idea to consult with a tax professional or financial planner for advice tailored to your specific situation.

Tax-Efficient Investing Strategies

Tax-efficient investing is a crucial part of retirement planning. It involves organizing and managing your investments in a way that reduces the taxes you pay and, as a result, increases your after-tax returns. Here are several strategies to consider:

Utilize Tax-Advantaged Retirement Accounts:

Maximize your contributions to tax-advantaged retirement accounts like 401(k)s, IRAs, and Roth IRAs. Contributions to traditional 401(k)s and traditional IRAs are generally tax-deductible, reducing your current taxable income. However, withdrawals in retirement are taxed as ordinary income.

On the other hand, contributions to Roth 401(k)s and Roth IRAs are made with after-tax dollars, so there is no immediate tax deduction. But, all withdrawals, including earnings, are generally tax-free in retirement, given certain conditions are met.

Asset Location:

Consider the tax efficiency of your investments when deciding where to hold them. High tax-efficiency investments, such as index funds and ETFs that generate mainly capital gains, can be held in taxable accounts. Investments that generate a lot of taxable income, such as bond funds or REITs, may be better held in tax-advantaged accounts.

Tax-Efficient Mutual Funds or ETFs:

Choose tax-efficient investment vehicles. For instance, index mutual funds and ETFs are usually more tax-efficient than actively managed funds because they turn over their portfolios less frequently, leading to fewer taxable capital gains distributions.

Tax-Loss Harvesting:

This strategy involves selling investments that have declined in value to offset the taxes on gains from other investments. You can then reinvest the proceeds into a similar but not identical investment to maintain your portfolio's balance and expected returns.

Hold Investments Longer:

Long-term capital gains rates are usually lower than short-term rates. So, holding investments for more than a year before selling can lower your tax bill.

Gift and Inheritance Strategies:

Consider gift and inheritance tax strategies. You may be able to gift shares of investments to family members in lower tax brackets or donate to charity. Also, under current tax laws, investments held until death receive a step-up in cost basis, potentially reducing taxes for heirs.

Required Minimum Distributions (RMDs):

Make sure you understand the rules about Required Minimum Distributions from retirement accounts. Failure to take out these distributions can result in high tax penalties.

Each of these strategies can help improve the tax efficiency of your investment portfolio, but their effectiveness depends on your individual circumstances. Consult a tax professional or financial advisor to ensure you're implementing the strategies that best fit your situation and meet your retirement goals. Tax laws are complex and can change frequently, so it's important to stay informed and adjust your strategies as needed.

Estate Planning and Inheritance Tax Considerations

Estate planning is an essential part of retirement planning. It's about ensuring that your wealth is distributed according to your wishes and in the most tax-efficient way possible after your death. Let's look at key aspects of estate planning and inheritance tax considerations:

Understanding Inheritance Taxes:

Inheritance tax is a tax that a person needs to pay on money or property they have inherited after the death of a loved one. In the U.S., federal estate tax is imposed on the transfer of the "taxable estate" of a deceased person, over a certain amount called an exemption.

However, most people won't be subject to federal estate taxes, because, as of my knowledge cutoff in 2021, the federal estate tax exemption was $11.7 million per individual and $23.4 million for married couples. State-level estate or inheritance taxes may apply and can have much lower exemptions, so it's crucial to understand the rules in your specific state.

Writing a Will:

Your will is a legal document that sets out your wishes regarding the distribution of your assets and the care of any minor children. Dying without a valid will results in intestacy, and state laws will determine how your property is distributed. This may not align with your wishes, and could also lead to unfavorable tax consequences.

Trusts:

Trusts can be a valuable tool in estate planning. They can help you control how and when your heirs receive their inheritance, protect assets from creditors, and potentially reduce estate taxes. Different types of trusts include revocable living trusts, irrevocable trusts, credit shelter trusts, and generation-skipping trusts, each with its own tax implications and benefits.

Gifting During Your Lifetime:

One way to reduce your taxable estate is to gift assets to your heirs during your lifetime. As of 2021, you can gift up to $15,000 per year per individual without incurring federal gift tax or reducing your federal estate tax exemption. Spouses can combine their annual exclusions to gift up to $30,000 per individual per year.

Beneficiary Designations:

Ensure your beneficiary designations for retirement accounts and life insurance policies are current. These assets pass outside of your will, directly to the named beneficiaries, so it's crucial to keep these designations up to date.

Power of Attorney and Advance Healthcare Directive:

Estate planning also involves planning for potential incapacity. A durable power of attorney lets you designate someone to manage your finances if you become unable to do so. An advance healthcare directive allows you to specify your wishes for medical treatment if you're unable to communicate them yourself.

Professional Guidance:

Estate planning can be complex, especially when considering tax implications. Working with an estate planning attorney and a financial advisor can help ensure your plan meets your goals and minimizes the potential tax burden for your heirs.

Remember, estate planning isn't a one-time event. You should review and potentially revise your estate plan after significant life events or changes in estate and tax laws. Proper estate planning can provide peace of mind that your loved ones will be taken care of and your wishes respected after you're gone.

Chapter 11: Lifestyle Planning

Planning for Leisure, Travel, and Hobbies in Retirement

While it's essential to focus on the financial aspects of retirement planning, it's equally crucial to consider how you want to spend your time in retirement. The decisions you make about leisure, travel, and hobbies can have a significant impact on your overall retirement budget and your quality of life. Here are some key considerations:

Envision Your Ideal Retirement:

Imagine what a typical day, week, or year might look like in your retirement. Do you see yourself traveling the world, spending time with family, engaging in hobbies, volunteering, or even starting a small business? Understanding what you want out of retirement can help you prepare financially and emotionally for this significant life change.

Budget for Leisure and Hobbies:

While some activities, like reading or gardening, may require minimal additional expenditure, others, like golf or traveling, can significantly impact your retirement budget. Try to quantify the potential cost of your hobbies and include them in your retirement budget. You might need to prioritize or find lower-cost alternatives depending on your overall financial situation.

Travel Planning:

Travel is a common aspiration for many retirees. Whether you want to visit family, explore new places, or even live part-time in a different location, travel costs can add up quickly. Consider how you want to travel, where you want to go, and how often. Don't forget to factor in expenses like airfare, accommodations, dining, activities, travel insurance, and health care costs while traveling.

Health and Fitness:

Physical activity is a vital aspect of maintaining health and wellbeing in retirement. You might want to join a gym, take up a sport, or invest in home fitness equipment. Consider these costs in your retirement budget and think about how to maintain an active lifestyle in a way that suits you.

Lifelong Learning:

Retirement is a great time to learn new things, whether for personal interest or to aid in your hobbies. You might want to take art classes, learn a new language, or even pursue an academic course. Many community colleges and universities offer discounted or free classes for seniors, so it's worth exploring your options.

Social Connections:

Maintaining social connections is critical for emotional health in retirement. This might involve regular outings with friends, participating in community groups, volunteering, or even part-time work. While some of these activities may have associated costs, others can also provide opportunities to enrich your life without impacting your budget significantly.

Be Flexible:

Finally, remember that your interests and abilities might change over time, so it's good to remain flexible. Have a range of activities you enjoy and be open to trying new things. A satisfying retirement is about more than just money; it's about enjoying your time and living a fulfilling life.

Remember, retirement is a significant life transition, and it's about more than just stopping work. It's about starting a new phase of life that can be as rewarding and exciting as you make it. So, while you're diligently saving and investing for retirement, also take the time to plan for how you want to spend your time in retirement.

Estimating Your Retirement "Paycheck"

One of the keys to a successful and stress-free retirement is being able to predict, with a fair degree of accuracy, your retirement "paycheck." This is the income you'll have to cover your living expenses during retirement. Here's how you can estimate it:

Identify Your Retirement Income Sources:

Your retirement income will likely come from a variety of sources. Here are some common ones:

- Social Security: You can estimate your future benefits using the Social Security Administration's online calculator.
- Pensions: If you have a defined benefit plan, your employer can provide an estimate of your monthly benefit.
- Retirement Accounts: Include any income from 401(k) plans, IRAs, and other tax-advantaged retirement accounts. How much income you can safely withdraw each year depends on various factors, including your account balances, age, and risk tolerance.
- Investments: Estimate the income from dividends, interest, and capital gains from your non-retirement investment accounts.
- Work: If you plan to work part-time, include the estimated income from this work.
- Other Sources: Include any other sources of income, such as rental income, annuities, business income, etc.

Calculate Your Total Annual Income:

Add up the income from all these sources to calculate your total annual retirement income. If some of your income sources are not guaranteed, like investment income, it might be prudent to estimate conservatively.

Compare Your Income to Your Expenses:

Once you've calculated your annual retirement income, compare this to your expected annual retirement expenses. If your income covers your expenses, you're in a good position. If not, you might need to adjust your plans, which could involve delaying retirement, reducing expenses, saving more, or considering other income sources.

Don't Forget Inflation:

Over time, inflation will erode the purchasing power of your money. A cost-of-living increase is often included in Social Security benefits and some pensions, but you'll need to consider inflation in other areas of your retirement planning.

Factor in Taxes:

Remember, your retirement income might be subject to taxes. This includes income tax on withdrawals from traditional 401(k)s and IRAs, capital gains tax on some investment income, and potentially taxes on Social Security benefits, depending on your total income.

Estimating your retirement "paycheck" can give you a clearer picture of your financial readiness for retirement. It's important to revisit these calculations periodically as your income, savings, and assumptions about retirement may change. With careful planning, you can aim to create a predictable income stream that will support your desired lifestyle throughout retirement.

Working in Retirement: Pros and Cons

Choosing to work in retirement is a personal decision that can have both financial and lifestyle implications. Here are some potential advantages and disadvantages to consider:

Pros of Working in Retirement:

Supplemental Income:

The most apparent benefit of working in retirement is the additional income. This can help cover living expenses, reduce the amount you need to withdraw from savings, or allow for extra spending on travel and hobbies.

Social Interaction:

Work provides an opportunity to interact with others and maintain social connections, which can contribute to emotional wellbeing in retirement.

Intellectual Stimulation:

Work can provide mental stimulation and a sense of purpose. This can be especially true if you're working in a field you're passionate about, or using skills you've developed over your career.

Health Benefits:

Some part-time or full-time jobs may offer health benefits, which can help cover medical costs. Plus, staying active and engaged can have positive health effects.

Longer Savings:

Working in retirement allows you to keep building your nest egg, delay drawing down your retirement savings, and possibly delay claiming Social Security, which can increase your benefits.

Cons of Working in Retirement:

Less Free Time:

Working in retirement means less time for other activities. This could impact your ability to travel, spend time with family, or pursue hobbies.

Job Market:

Depending on your field, finding satisfying work in retirement might be challenging. Age discrimination, despite being illegal, is still a problem in some industries.

Impact on Benefits:

Earning too much can impact the taxation of your Social Security benefits and push you into a higher tax bracket. It's essential to understand these implications before deciding to work in retirement.

Health Considerations:

If you have health issues, working in retirement might be physically demanding or stressful. It's crucial to find a balance between work and maintaining your health.

Mental Wellbeing:

While some people thrive on work, others might find it stressful or tiring. Retirement should be a time of enjoyment, and if work becomes a source of unhappiness, it might not be worth it.

In conclusion, choosing to work in retirement is a personal decision that depends on your financial needs, health, and how you wish to spend your time. Some retirees find working provides them with many benefits beyond just income, while others prefer to focus on leisure, hobbies, and family. As with all aspects of retirement planning, it's all about finding what works best for you.

Chapter 12: Staying Financially Secure in Retirement

How to Adjust Your Strategy Over Time

Retirement is not a static period of life but a dynamic journey with different stages. As you progress through retirement, your needs, priorities, and circumstances can change. Therefore, maintaining financial security throughout retirement often requires periodic adjustments to your financial strategy. Here's how you can do it:

Regular Review of Your Portfolio:

Regularly review your investment portfolio to ensure it aligns with your current risk tolerance, income needs, and financial goals. The mix of assets that worked for you at the beginning of retirement might not be ideal later on. For example, you might need to adjust your asset allocation to generate more income or to reduce risk as you age.

Adjusting Withdrawal Rates:

Your annual withdrawal rate from your retirement accounts might need to be adjusted over time. Factors that might require an adjustment include significant changes in the value of your portfolio, changes in your living expenses, or a desire to leave a larger or smaller estate to heirs.

Rethinking Risk:

Early in retirement, you might have been comfortable taking on more investment risk to achieve growth. But as you age, preserving capital might become a higher priority. Reducing investment risk might involve shifting assets into more conservative investments or using financial products designed to provide guaranteed income.

Adapting to Life Changes:

Major life events, like the loss of a spouse, a significant health event, or changes in your housing situation, can necessitate significant adjustments in your financial strategy.

Estate Planning Review:

As you age, estate planning can become more relevant. Regular reviews of your estate plan are crucial to ensure it aligns with your current wishes, tax laws, and family situation.

Adjusting for Inflation:

The cost of living will likely increase over time due to inflation. Your income needs to keep pace with this to maintain your buying power. This might involve cost-of-living adjustments in your budget, investments that provide inflation protection, or annuities with inflation adjustment features.

Regular Health Care Planning:

Healthcare needs often increase as one ages, so it's crucial to revisit your healthcare plans regularly. Make sure you understand and are prepared for the potential costs of long-term care, should you require it.

Tax Implications:

As tax laws and your income sources change, so might your tax situation. Regularly review this with a tax advisor to ensure you're not paying more tax than necessary.

In conclusion, maintaining financial security in retirement is an ongoing process. By regularly reviewing and adjusting your financial strategy, you can adapt to changing circumstances and help ensure a comfortable and secure retirement.

Handling Market Volatility in Retirement

Market volatility can be particularly stressful for retirees, who often rely on their investments for income. While it's impossible to eliminate investment risk entirely, here are some strategies to help manage market volatility in retirement:

Diversification:

Having a diversified portfolio spread across different asset classes, sectors, and geographic regions can help cushion the blow of market downturns. If one asset class is performing poorly, others might be doing well. Regularly rebalance your portfolio to maintain your desired level of diversification.

Asset Allocation:

The mix of stocks, bonds, and cash in your portfolio plays a significant role in determining its risk level. As a general rule, as you age, you might want to reduce your exposure to stocks, which are typically more volatile, and increase your holdings in more stable investments like bonds and cash.

Maintain a Cash Reserve:

Having a cash reserve can provide income during periods of market downturn, so you're not forced to sell investments at depressed prices. A common rule of thumb is to have enough cash to cover at least one to two years of living expenses.

Use Dividends and Interest for Income:

If you rely on your investments for income, consider strategies that focus on generating income from dividends and interest rather than selling assets. This approach can provide a steady income stream and reduce the need to sell during a market downturn.

Annuities:

Certain types of annuities can provide a guaranteed income stream regardless of market conditions. However, annuities can be complex and may have high fees, so they're not suitable for everyone.

Stay the Course:

Market downturns can be unnerving, but it's essential to avoid making rash decisions based on fear. Stick to your investment plan unless your circumstances or goals have changed. Remember, market downturns are often followed by recoveries.

Seek Professional Advice:

A financial advisor can help you design an investment strategy that fits your risk tolerance and income needs. They can also provide guidance during periods of market volatility and help prevent emotional decision-making.

Remember, while these strategies can help manage risk, they can't eliminate it entirely. Every investment involves some degree of risk, and it's essential to understand this before investing. The key is to find a balance that allows for potential growth while protecting your assets to the degree that you're comfortable with.

Estate Planning and Leaving a Financial Legacy

Estate planning is a crucial part of retirement planning, especially if you wish to leave a financial legacy for your loved ones or make a charitable impact. Not only does it ensure that your assets are distributed according to your wishes, but it also has potential tax implications that could affect the amount that your beneficiaries receive. Here's a closer look:

Draft a Will:

A will is the cornerstone of any estate plan, outlining how you wish to distribute your assets after your death. If you die without a valid will, the state will determine the distribution of your assets according to its laws, which might not align with your wishes.

Set Up Beneficiaries:

Ensure that your retirement accounts, insurance policies, and other financial accounts have up-to-date beneficiary designations. These designations typically override any instructions in a will, so it's crucial to keep them current.

Establish Trusts:

Trusts can be used for a variety of purposes, such as reducing estate taxes, protecting assets from creditors, or controlling how and when beneficiaries receive their inheritance. A revocable living trust, for example, allows your estate to avoid probate, a public and often time-consuming legal process.

Consider Life Insurance:

Life insurance can provide a tax-free lump sum to your beneficiaries upon your death, which can be particularly useful if your estate is largely tied up in non-liquid assets, like real estate.

Charitable Giving:

If you wish to leave a legacy to a charity, there are several ways to do this, from simply leaving a bequest in your will to setting up a charitable trust.

Power of Attorney and Advance Medical Directives:

Estate planning is not just about what happens after your death. A durable power of attorney, healthcare proxy, and living will allow others to make financial and medical decisions on your behalf if you become unable to do so yourself.

Estate Taxes:

While estate taxes won't affect everyone, if your estate exceeds certain thresholds, a substantial portion could go to taxes rather than your beneficiaries. Strategies like gifting during your lifetime or setting up trusts can help minimize this liability.

Professional Guidance:

Estate planning can be complex, and laws vary by state and country. Work with an attorney who specializes in estate planning to ensure your plan is legally sound and achieves your goals.

In conclusion, proper estate planning allows you to leave a financial legacy for your loved ones and causes you care about. It provides the peace of mind that your wishes will be carried out and that you've done your best to protect your beneficiaries from unnecessary costs and delays.

Chapter 13: Conclusion

As we draw this comprehensive guide on retirement planning and wealth management to a close, let's take a moment to revisit the key insights we've gleaned throughout our journey.

Retirement planning is an ongoing process that requires continuous effort, adaptation, and foresight. From understanding the significance of early planning to adjusting strategies over time, every step in this process is equally critical and interlinked.

We've learned how to evaluate our financial status, keeping an eye on our net worth and the impact of debt on our financial plans. We've also discovered the importance of establishing clear and flexible retirement goals and implementing the right strategies for saving and investing to meet those goals.

We've navigated through the world of investing, diversifying our portfolios, and balancing risk and return. We've understood how to leverage different retirement-specific investment options, the role of social security and pensions, and how to manage healthcare costs in retirement.

Our journey has shed light on how real estate can impact our retirement planning, tax implications of retirement income, and how to plan our lifestyle in retirement. We've also learned about the importance of staying financially secure throughout our retirement and the significance of estate planning and leaving a financial legacy.

Remember, your retirement should be a time of relaxation, enjoyment, and the pursuit of passions that you couldn't accommodate during your working years. To ensure a comfortable and secure retirement, start planning today, invest wisely, save diligently, and maintain a level-headed approach towards market volatility.

The journey to a rich retirement is unique for each of us. What remains constant, however, is the importance of informed, mindful, and proactive planning.

As your journey unfolds, may you find your path enriched by the insights and strategies discussed in this book. Here's to a future where each one of us can retire rich and enjoy the fruits of our hard-earned labor. Here's to a future where our golden years are truly golden.

Thank you for joining me on this journey through "Retire Rich: Planning for a Comfortable Retirement". Here's to your prosperous future and a retirement filled with joy, comfort, and financial peace of mind.